Gold Investing & Trading Guide: Gold & Silver Bullion Buying Trader's Guide with Pro Gold Investment Tips & Hacks

Jon Dallas

Published by InfinitYou, 2017.

GOLD INVESTING & TRADING GUIDE: GOLD & SILVER BULLION BUYING TRADER'S GUIDE WITH PRO GOLD INVESTMENT TIPS & HACKS

First edition. July 11, 2017.

ISBN: 978-1386821731

Written by Jon Dallas.

Favorite Quote About Gold

"As fewer and fewer people have confidence in paper as a store of value, the price of gold will continue to rise."

—Jerome F. Smith

Introduction

The objective of this book is to narrow down your options and find the perfect gold investment way for your personal financial situation.

Here are some introductory facts that you should know about gold before we get started.

Gold is the most popular metal as an investment. It is the most precious metals of all known to the human kind. One can purchase the precious metal of gold as a hedge or as a harbor against political, economic, or social fiat currency crises. This includes investment market declines, currency failure, burgeoning national debt, war, inflation, or social instabilities.

The gold market as any other market is subject to speculation, especially through the use of derivatives and futures contracts.

Investors who went through the experience of the 2007-2012 global financial crisis suggest that gold behaves more like a currency than a commodity.

Another interesting thing that you might find interesting about gold is the fact that gold is a soft, dense, shiny, ductile, and malleable metal. It is also a chemical element with the symbol Au and the atomic number 79. The melting point of gold is

1,064 °C and the boiling point is 2,856 °C. The atomic mass of gold is 196.96657 ± 0.00004 u.

Some More Facts About Gold:

1. Gold is the most popular and highest trading metal all over the globe.

2. Given that gold is the highest trading metal, the amount of gold traded in the marketplace is very high and therefore there exists the tendency of very low risk.

3. Gold enjoys a series of very special tax exception in most of the countries around the globe.

4. Investing in gold is a very effective protection agains the inflation.

5. An investment in gold is the best form of an investment for people with limited funds. Gold is the perfect investment for individuals who are looking for the assured profits on their investment. A beginner who is going to invest in gold should be following the standard safeguards in buying and selling of this precious metal which will ensure an assured profit of the gold investment.

Gold A Newbie Buying Opportunity

Have you ever thought of investing in gold? Well, gold provides a good opportunity for new investors to put money into well thought out investments. The demand for gold keeps on increasing each day with more and more money available worldwide. This fact makes inflation inevitable. There are many ways through which a new gold investor can invest in the most precious metal of gold. Each different method for gold investment has their advantages and disadvantages.

Gold is also the precious metal that has recently experienced a great extent of renewed interest. The physical gold can actually be used in so many different ways. This fact makes investing in gold a very lucrative business for new investors.

However, one important aspect of investing in gold is to comprehend that gold investment comes in two basic forms. The first is trading with the physical gold and the second is trading gold in the stock market.

These two forms of gold investments are both profitable, but they are different in so many ways.

Investing in gold is one of the most effective ways to hedge against inflation and to build up a stronger portfolio. There are ,however, some critical facts that should be given high preference and that you should absolutely know about as a new gold investor. Be aware that investing is one thing and making profit from it is another thing.

The best investment opportunities for a new investor can still be made with gold and this is why I put this guide together for you.

Gold is among the most precious investment options that are available and open to you as a new investor.

The goal of this guide is to show you 9 profitable ways how you can do just this so that you will be able to choose your favorite gold investing way once you are done going through this guide.

Investing in gold provides a bigger challenge for beginners since it is somehow risky if you don't know the market and how to invest the correct way. For a beginner, there are many ways open in today's marketplace.

The challenge comes with choosing the one way that makes sense for the individual investor because it is going to also depend on factors like personal preferences, budget, financial situation, and many more factors.

This guide shows you the top nine ways to choose from if you are a new to gold investing. The guide is meant to provide a new investor with a general overview of all the ways that are available for a new investor. I have picked them in an effort to provide you with the best mix and the widest variety of ways that you can choose to profit from.

You are in no way limited to these 9 ways because there are many more ways available to invest in gold.

The goal here is to provide a new gold investor with the most valuable, usable, and easy to consume information and this is why I decided to stick to the top 9 ways.

I feel that information overload is doing you harm because a cluttered mind is a mind that does not take action.

The goal is simply to get a general overview of the top ways and top opportunities and to pick one as a starting point and to move to the next step.

This way you will get a basic overview of the opportunity without getting stuck and you are able to move on and quickly proceed to the actual trading action.

The real fun begins once you are able to pick your favorite gold trading way.

Once you have identified the way that you want to stick to, you can proceed to the section The Next Step.

Be aware that I will constantly be updating this book so that it will always reflect the top ways and opportunities for a beginner to invest in gold so make sure to check for updates regularly. I will inform you about the latest updates on my Facebook page, too.

Please make sure to look at the New Releases section to get to my Facebook page and to check out my latest releases in this investing for beginner's series.

Please also refer to the 30+ Gold Investing Resources section of this book to learn continue your gold investing learning path and learn about more gold investing opportunities as you move forward with your gold investment.

Let's move on with the top nine ways a beginner could invest in gold.

First Way: Buying Physical Gold

Today, the best investment for a beginning investor is to make in gold. Gold is among the most precious investment options available to investors around the globe. For new investors, investing in gold provides a bigger challenge since it is somehow risky. As a new investor you need to make sure to know the marketplace and the know how. For a new gold investor, there are many ways to pick from. Here is the first way a beginner could invest in gold.

Physical gold is available in many parts of the globe. Beginners can choose from a variety of ways like buying gold jewelry, buying gold coins, and buying gold bullions. The best investment falls in the sector of buying gold bullions. The golden bullions are more affordable for new investors. They have lower costs associated and have higher liquidation values. This means the gold bullions are sold easily at a very high price when they are placed on the marketplace within a short time period. Another advantage of buying gold bullions is the availability in different forms. This includes a bullion coin that also acts as legal tenders in specific countries around the globe.

If you choose to buy gold coins and bars, new investors have to pay high prices. The small gold bars make it difficult to refine in factories. For those storing physical gold, they have to put security measures up to the standard. Before buying any physical gold as an investment, it is required that you verify the purity of the physical gold. The vaulted gold that is stored is affordable as an investment and has a high liquidity plan.

The actual process of investing in physical gold goes like this. Investing in physical gold is the process of buying actual gold which could be in the form of coins or bars.

This type of investment is best if an investor wants an asset that is stable in value. The gold coins and bars are bought and kept at the bank or in a safe at home.

The physical gold is a means of preserving wealth that appreciates in value and over time. Gold is a recognized international currency. Physical possession of gold enables the investor to trade it globally.

The ownership of the gold means that one has the equivalent in money and can use it whenever needed.

A visit to a gold seller who is licensed and certified will suffice to get the coins or bars. Always be on the lookout to avoid buying fake gold or being overcharged.

Gold is a long term option and not a revenue generating option for the short term. The draw backs of investing in physical gold are the security and insurance measures that are needed to safeguard it.

This brings us to the next related chapter of physical gold. You will learn more about gold bars as a form of physical gold and as a very profitable way of investing in gold.

Second Way: Investing In Gold Bars

Gold investing in bars is considered a primitive way of trading with gold. However, gold investing in bars is still a relevant method that still works today.

Historically, this method involved selling and buying physical gold.

A gold investor can buy precious metals like gold in the marketplace where the prize is low and then the investor can sell it on another marketplace where the prize is higher.

With this method, the investor will be able to accumulate a lot of cash from the profits. The investor will make the profits with the sales of the gold.

If you opt in for this gold bar buying way, you only have to make sure of one thing. You have to make sure that you buy the gold from a marketplace where prizes for gold are low. You have to identify a marketplace where you can sell your gold at a higher prize.

The gold bars come in different sizes, too. Gold is available in small 1 oz bars or larger bars.

You can invest in gold bars where you physically own gold. This is an effective and common way you can invest in gold as a newbie.

The gold bar is an iconic image of investing in physical gold. In most countries gold bars are sold by major banks in quantities that are standardized. It is easy to get them if you have the right documentation and money to purchase the required quantity.

If you decided to use gold bars, you own them as assets. This is advantageous because there is no risk of default as it is happening with paper asset.

Third Way: Gold Investing In Coins

The third way that a beginner could invest in gold is called gold investment in coins. This can happen in the form of bullion coins or in the form of collection gold coins.

Applying this method can be very profitable for the gold investor. It can be more profitable than you might think.

Why?

The value of the coins might exceed their gold weight value. This can stand out to be more profitable than you might think as the value of the coin might exceed the gold weight value.

With regards to the history and the origin of gold coins, it is likely that it may cost more than the actual gold weight value that is contained in it.

Another way you can invest in gold is by the use of gold bullion coins. Gold is mostly traded in the form of gold coins with the most popular one being Krugerrand.

The Krugerrand occupies almost ninety percent of the gold coin market. There are also numismatic gold coins available that have the value of the gold they contain.

There are also various trading organizations and certification agencies that give a guarantee of the authenticity and grade

of the gold coins.

You have the option to buy the quantity you want and you can also buy and sell gold coins online.

Fourth Way: Gold Mining Funds And Stocks

When looking for an investment opportunity for gold as a beginning investor, you can look at the gold mining fund or stock in the marketplaces. Gold mining funds or stock is not hard to find as compared to physical gold. You can find a forum through which beginners can invest in securities and give them exposure.

With gold mining funds and stocks you do not invest directly in physical gold, but you get an opportunity to invest in shares of companies trading in gold or mining companies.

Remember that the price of gold in the marketplace influences the price set by the mining stock companies. Other factors to look at do include the company owners, the management, the reserves available, and many other variables.

In order to spread the risk of getting losses, new gold investors must make sure to do the proper research first and to put the invested money into different gold mining companies.

Any fund for investment placed on several different companies automatically reduces losses of investment. However, a beginner must know that you do not really own real gold in this investment portfolio. You own the shares of these gold mining companies only. Sometimes, shares can lose value over time just like the physical gold could drop in price, too.

Gold mining funds and stocks are a very viable way to invest in gold as a newbie. This helps you to increase your exposure to gold. The mining companies also assist you to invest the gold and therefore if you do not have much experience with trading gold funds and stocks there is no need to worry for you.

You just need to invest in the companies that have good reputation in investing in the stocks in order to be guaranteed a high return on investment.

Fifth Way: Gold Options & Futures

This is the fifth way of how a newbie investor could invest in gold.

Gold options and futures are for the investor who is speculative in nature and who opts to buy cheap and sell at higher prices later. Investing like this requires a lot of tact and expert opinion. It is a risky investment option because one could incur losses instead of making money. This option, however, allows investors with little funds to control large investments.

This way of gold investment is very profitable because in most cases, prices keep on increasing in the world markets.

A newbie should consider gold futures and options as yet another method of investing in gold.

With this method, the investor, though not experienced, speculates on the market price of gold. This, however, goes either way. For example, by getting the call, you are sure the market price rises. The call is used to fix the buying price.

If the price rises, buyers get a bigger margin on fixed options and the day trading price. For those investing and choosing to buy the put, they are expecting for the price to fall.

However, this is a somehow risky way to buy these options. For the new beginner trying to start an investment in gold, buying gold option and futures requires help from an experienced advisor who knows how the market of gold options and futures behaves.

The best trait about this is the fact that an investor controls a big investment with little cash. The bad trait, however, is that these options expire after a fixed period. Therefore, when investing using this method, make sure that you are careful with timing. Always get advice from a trained financial advisor whom you can trust and ask for more information about gold options and futures.

This is by far the most difficult way for a beginner to invest in gold, and I recommend to stay away from this method if you do not know what you are doing. I do not want to leave this way of trading gold out of the big picture.

I want to show you the full spectrum of gold investing ways so that you get an overview of the most important gold investing methods and to let you know about all the options that are open to you as a gold investor.

Gold options and futures are certainly a good way for the advanced gold investor who is looking for another profitable gold investing opportunity to add to his or her portfolio.

Sixth Way: Gold Exchange Trade Funds (ETFs)

Here is the sixth way a beginner could invest in gold.

If you are a new investor trying a hand in this gold exchange trade funds portfolio, this provides the best opportunity for investment for a newbie.

In recent months, there has been an increase in the ETFs. The ETF is a fund which allows trading in stock markets just like the ordinary shares. The unique thing about this is that the portfolios of the ETF are fixed and remain constant.

The trading companies that are dealing with the ETF do posses the gold bullions as an asset. This means you can check their symbols and identify them either as GLD or IAU.

This ETF gold exchange trade funds opportunity offers new investors an opportunity to invest in gold and make good profits this way.

This is by the way the best option for those who are uncomfortable with storing and owning physical metal. Gold Exchange Trade Funds are are special in that they track the gold spot and they are mainly traded in the main stock exchanges like the Paris, London, Zurich, New York and Tokyo stock exchange.

The main disadvantage of this investment is the management fee that comes with it. You will be charged by the company issuing the ETFs. A 0.4% commission for trading in gold ETFs is charged on top of the annual storage fee, too.

Seventh Way: COMEX Gold Investment

Another way of owning and investing gold for a newbie is the COMEX gold contract options way. The COMEX gold contract options are real contracts which help specifying the future gold deliveries at a fixed prize.

The future deliveries are then used for speculations on the actual prizes based on the lowest prize of physical gold that you as an investor posses.

In America for example, using the COMEX investment option in future contracts is set and standardized. It deals with the future exchange. The investor is buying gold future in the contract which is locking future deliveries in terms of quality and quantity.

When the investor buys the future contracts in gold, the benefit comes when the prize rises above the contract futures.

However, sellers only gain when there are lower prizes. The trick with this kind of investment is to buy these futures based on margins by having smaller secured deposits in the investment accounts. This method is very secure and helps against losses.

Eights Way: Online Gold Trading

With online gold trading a new investor can trade with an investment fund that is traded on stock exchanges, like it is done with stocks. This is a business of trading in the financial marketplace. The method allows new investors to invest in gold without physically purchasing the gold and without having to store it. The investor trades with it by buying shares of ETF in an online brokerage account.

However, if a beginner plans to trade efficiently on this kind of platform, it will be necessary to have access to gold sport prizes on a daily basis.

In addition, the investor must first employ the service and trust of a true financial professional in the stock market, to help with the necessary guidelines to start with the actual trading process.

Investing in gold online, can only be profitable when you as the investor are familiar with the necessary skills, know-how, and tools. Online gold trading takes the proper knowledge in order to be able to take proper action.

Besides, you will also require some necessary trading tools, rules, and guidelines, which can be provided by your trusted advisor that you have choosen beforehand.

It is mandatory for all beginners to first start with tutorials and training. As a beginning investor you must absolutely be familiar with all the necessary trading alerts and tools that you are going to need for a safe gold investment that guarantees some god profits.

This is the reason why I included an additional resources section at the end of this book where you can go through additional gold investing resources, additional information, and gold investing kits and tutorials and learn more about the safest and most profitable ways of gold investing and how to go from there to make it happen.

Please proceed to the Resources section whenever you feel ready for it because this is the section where you will find some specific resources and instructions for beginners who are looking to invest in gold and once you have accumulated enough knowledge you can seek professional advice from a trusted source or advisor and proceed from there to the actual online trading process.

Ninth Way: E-Gold

The ninth and last way of gold trading is called E-gold or electronic gold trading. E-gold is a good gold investment option offered by licensed national institutions. This method involves a national owned electronic way of investing in gold and hence the name E-gold.

Trading with E-gold is a transparent way of market investment for beginning investors because it allows for risk free facilities.

With this way of investing in gold, a beginner is allowed to invest in small denominations. Smaller denominations involve

1 gram or other forms.

This specific E-gold method of investing in gold is similar to the equities cash segments. It is required that a new investor opens a trading account at the national institution. Each unit of electronic gold that is purchased equals 1 gram of gold.

The E-gold trading is backed by the quantity of gold that is kept safely at the appropriate storage facility.

Conclusion

The goal of this book is to cover the 9 top ways of investing in gold. Hopefully by now this goal is met and you got an overall overview of all the ways that are available to you.

By now, you should also be aware of one very critical and important aspect of gold investments. You as the beginner need to understand that gold investment comes in two basic forms.

Form one involes trading with the physical gold and form two involves trading gold in the stock market. Both forms of gold investments and trading with gold are profitable, but at the same time they are very different in many ways.

As you have been able to see going through the nine different ways of investing in gold, there is a true opportunity today with gold that you as a beginner should take advantage of.

For beginners, investing in gold provides a big challenge, too. You should always be aware of the opportunity and the risks at the same time.

These top nine ways of investing in gold should only be used as a guide to show you all the options and opportunities that are available to you on today's marketplace.

Once you have picked your favorite way that reflects your own budget and your financial situation, I highly recommend to you to dig deeper into the research about that specific way and seek more professional advice before actually going ahead and investing right away.

It is extremely important for you to do your homework thoroughly before actually entering the market.

Once you pick your favorite way of gold investment, you can go ahead and use it as a starting point for further research that you can do on your own via the resources section in this book.

The resources section is where you can continue your research specifically for the gold investing method that you like to get started with for now.

In addition, this research will help you identify a professional advisor who will be able to point you into the right direction depending on your choosen gold investing way and your financial situation and goal.

Once you feel ready after having done your proper research, I recommend first seeking the help of a professional advisor who you can trust and who is an expert in your choosen way of investing in gold. For example, if you picked gold mining funds and stocks you should look for an online or offline expert who can guide you into the right direction from where you can get started with the actual investing process of gold mining funds and stock, etc.

I hope you enjoyed going through this overall guide that has shown you the 9 top ways a beginner could invest in gold. I hope that you are encouraged, excited and motivated about this gold investing opportunity that is open to you.

It is up to you to identify and pick your own favorite way. Go ahead and use it as a starting point for further exploration into this exciting and very profitable opportunity of investing in gold.

I wish you all the best success with your gold financing goals.

To your success with gold investing!

The Next Step

In order to learn more about the additional important and critical aspects that you needs to know about investing in gold, I have included 30+ Gold Investing Resource for you that will help you narrow down your options and guide you through the process before actually doing it.

Once you have gone through all the resources, key questions, and methods that are outlined via the resources section, you will be able to gather enough information about the gold investing way that you picked from the nine ways.

During this research process, you will be able to identify a trusted online or offline expert that will be able to help you move forward and put together a personalized gold investing plan of action for you that is going to fit your budget and your personal financial situation.

So I hope by now you have picked your favorite way of investing in gold. If so, you can go ahead to the next step of the journey which is the research phase.

Go to the 30+ Gold Investing Resources section in the next chapter to get started with your next step and once you will have gathered enough information and a trusted source, you will be able to get into the real action...

Ah, and one more thing, as a surprise bonus, I have included a fun little quiz for you in order to test your basic knowledge of what you have learned so far.

To get started with the quiz just proceed to the Quiz section and look for 12 basic gold investing terms in order to solve the quiz.

Get a sheet of paper and give yourself enough space to write down the 12 gold investment terms that you should be looking for.

You can be very creative and look for the terms that are written in all kinds of directions and not only from left to right. Keep looking from up to down and vice versa.

If you are stuck, keep looking from the perspective of all possible directions that you can think of.

I hope these little hints help you solve the quiz and write down the 12 basic gold investing terms on your piece of paper.

Once you are done, you can verify if your answers are correct by looking up the answers in the next chapter that is titled Quiz Results.

You can play this game with a friend or with a group of people and you can make it more exciting by rewarding the winner with a nice treat.

Good luck with the quiz and I wish you a very successful next step in your gold investing journey!

30+ Gold Investing Resources

Free Gold Kit[1]

How To Invest In Gold[2]
http://www.goldprice.org[3]
http://www.bullionvault.com[4]
http://www.organogold.com[5]
http://www.investopedia.com[6]
http://www.seekingalpha.com[7]
http://www.wikinvest.com[8]
http://www.fool.com[9]
http://www.mint.com[10]
http://www.moneysavingexpert.com[11]
http://www.goldprice.org[12]
http://www.investopedia.com[13]
http://www.seekingalpha.com[14]
http://www.theaureport.com[15]
http://onlygold.com[16]
http://www.gold.org[17]
http://www.321gold.com[18]
http://www.bulliondirect.com[19]

---

1. http://www.answerszone.info/fast-udemy-cash/regalassets-free-gold-kit
2. http://answerszone.info/fast-udemy-cash/resources
3. http://www.goldprice.org/
4. http://www.bullionvault.com/
5. http://www.organogold.com/
6. http://www.investopedia.com/
7. http://seekingalpha.com/
8. http://www.wikinvest.com/
9. http://www.fool.com/
10. http://www.mint.com/
11. http://www.moneysavingexpert.com/
12. http://www.goldprice.org/
13. http://www.investopedia.com/
14. http://seekingalpha.com/
15. http://www.theaureport.com/
16. http://onlygold.com/
17. http://www.gold.org/
18. http://www.321gold.com/
19. http://www.bulliondirect.com/

http://www.goldseek.com[20]
http://www.gold-eagle.com[21]
https://wealthcycles.com[22]
http://www.galmarley.com/index.htm
http://www.sharelynx.com[23]
http://www.24hgold.com/english/home.aspx
http://www.golddealer.com[24]
http://www.safehaven.com[25]
http://www.kitco.com/charts/livegold.html
http://www.wikihow.com/Invest-in-Gold-and-Silver
http://www.ehow.com/how_2313812_invest-gold-silver-coins.html
http://www.consumer.ftc.gov/articles/0134-investing-gold

---

20. http://www.goldseek.com/
21. http://www.gold-eagle.com/
22. https://wealthcycles.com/
23. http://www.sharelynx.com/
24. http://www.golddealer.com/
25. http://www.safehaven.com/

Gold Quiz

Gold Quiz

J	H	K	U	X	U	M	O	E	W	M	E
I	U	A	B	D	Q	U	Y	V	K	U	K
K	G	P	F	N	V	I	C	R	Y	E	P
S	X	L	Y	A	C	D	N	E	B	C	V
R	Y	A	S	R	O	A	E	S	U	I	R
S	M	T	I	R	I	L	R	E	L	R	D
R	I	I	L	E	N	L	R	R	L	P	J
A	N	N	V	G	S	A	U	D	I	D	Q
B	I	U	E	U	L	P	C	L	O	L	K
E	N	M	R	R	A	Q	A	O	N	O	T
S	G	Y	R	K	U	R	C	G	R	G	G

Quiz Results

1. Gold price
2. Bars
3. Coins
4. Mining
5. Gold Reserve
6. Palladium
7. Platinum
8. Silver
9. Bullion
10. Currency
11. Krugerrand
12. Short Selling

About the Publisher

InfinitYou is a hybrid general interest trade publisher. One of the first of its kind InfinitYou publishes physical books, electronic books, and audiobooks in various genres. Our publications are meant to educate, edify and entertain readers of all walks of life from babies to the elderly.Home to more than twenty imprints such as Infinit Baby, Infinit Kids, Infinit Girl, Infinit Boy, Infinit Coloring, Infinit Swear Words, Infinit Activities, Infinit Productivity, Infinit Cat, Infinit Dog, Infinit Love, Infinit Family, Infinit Survival, Infinit Health, Infinit Beauty, Infinit Spirituality, Infinit Lifestyle, Infinit Wealth, Infinit Romance, and lots more.

9 783743 996663